An Illustrated Timeline of
INVENTIONS and INVENTORS

by Kremena T. Spengler
illustrated by Rick Morgan

PICTURE WINDOW BOOKS

a capstone imprint

Special thanks to our adviser, Terry Flaherty, PhD, Professor of English,
Minnesota State University, Mankato, for his expertise.

Editor: Jill Kalz
Designer: Tracy Davies
Art Director: Nathan Gassman
Production Specialist: Sarah Bennett
The illustrations in this book were created with pencil and digital color.

Photo Credits: Shutterstock: Andrea Danti, Diana Rich

Picture Window Books
151 Good Counsel Drive
P.O. Box 669
Mankato, MN 56002-0669
877-845-8392
www.capstonepub.com

All books published by Picture Window Books
are manufactured with paper containing at least
10 percent post-consumer waste.

Library of Congress Cataloging-in-Publication Data
Spcnglcr, Krcmcna.
  An illustrated timeline of inventions and inventors / by Kremena T.
Spengler ; illustrated by Rick Morgan.
    p. cm. — (Visual timelines in history)
  Includes index.
  ISBN 978-1-4048-6662-1 (library binding)
  ISBN 978-1-4048-7017-8 (paperback)
  1. Inventions—History—Chronology—Juvenile literature. 2.
Inventors—Biography—Juvenile literature. I. Morgan, Rick, 1954– ill.
II. Title.
  T48.S68 2012
  602'.02—dc22
                        2011010463

Printed in the United States of America, North Mankato, Minnesota
082011   006311R

Since earliest times, humans have tried to understand and change their surroundings. They have designed all sorts of tools to better their lives—from simple stone weapons to complex computers.

Millions of inventions exist. This book gives you a taste of some of the most interesting ones. Written as a timeline, it lists facts in the order in which they happened. Read the book from start to finish, or dip in and out! Discover at a glance who invented what. And see how one invention often led to another.

IN THE BEGINNING

ca. 1 million BC

Early humans learn to control fire. They use it to keep warm, cook food, and protect themselves against wild animals.

ca. 25,000 BC

People use needles and thread to make clothes.

ca. 70,000 BC

Stone Age humans learn to sharpen stones to make weapons.

ca. 15,000 BC

People invent the lunar calendar. They begin to record time based on the cycles, or phases, of the moon.

ca. 10,000 BC

The first clay pots are made.

ca. 5500 BC

Mesopotamians invent the plow. It helps farmers plant crops more easily.

ca. 6500 BC

The invention of weaving improves clothes making.

ca. 8700 BC

People in Mesopotamia make the first metal objects from copper.

ca. 3500 BC

Mesopotamians invent the wheel. Countless future inventions will rely on it.

ANCIENT CIVILIZATIONS

ca. 2500 BC

The ancient Egyptians develop glass.

ca. 2000 BC

The Minoans on the island of Crete create channels to deliver water over large distances. These channels are called aqueducts.

ca. 2000 BC

The first phonetic alphabet is developed in Egypt. Each symbol stands for a sound in the Egyptian language.

ca. 1500 BC

Egyptians invent the sundial. A sundial uses the light of the sun to tell time.

ca. 1000 BC

Mesopotamians invent the first calculator, called an abacus.

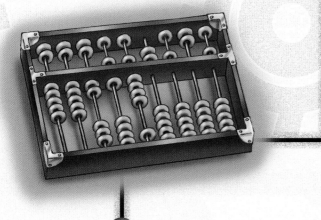

ca. 200 BC

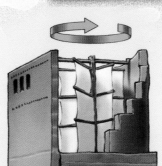

People in China and Persia build windmills to make use of wind power.

ca. 230 BC

Greek inventor Archimedes creates the compound pulley. A pulley makes it easier to lift heavy objects.

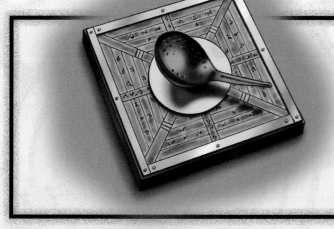

ca. 400 BC

The Chinese make the earliest compass.

THE PAPER TRAIL

▶ AD 105

The Chinese invent paper.

ca. 806

The Chinese begin using paper money.

ca. 800

The Chinese invent gunpowder.

ca. 1202

Italian mathematician Leonardo Pisano, known as Fibonacci, brings Arabic numerals to Europe. These numbers replace Roman numerals.

ca. 1300

The Chinese invent the musket, an early rifle.

ca. 1608

Dutch eyeglass maker Hans Lippershey invents the telescope. It helps people discover objects in the sky not seen with the naked eye.

ca. 1450

Johannes Gutenberg of Germany invents the printing press. With its movable type, the press makes large numbers of books easier and cheaper than before.

ca. 1590

Dutch craftsmen Hans and Zacharias Janssen invent an early microscope.

9

HEATING THINGS UP

1714

Daniel Gabriel Fahrenheit, a German physicist, invents the mercury thermometer. It provides a standard way to measure temperature.

1776

American David Bushnell builds the Turtle, an early submarine.

1742

American inventor Benjamin Franklin creates the Franklin Stove. It heats buildings in a safer, more efficient way than traditional fireplaces.

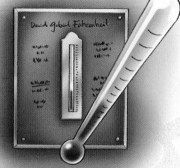

1765

Scottish engineer James Watt improves the steam engine, making it much more useful. Steam engines later power factories, train locomotives, and steamboats.

1783

On June 4, French brothers Joseph and Jacques Montgolfier fly the first hot air balloon.

1793

American Eli Whitney creates the cotton gin. It separates the seeds from the cotton fiber, saving time and energy.

1799

Italian physicist Alessandro Volta invents the battery. It's the first device to make its own electricity.

1783

French scientist Louis-Sebastien Lenormand invents the first working parachute.

1791

The French Academy of Sciences designs the metric system. The simple decimal system of measurement will be used around the world.

1796

English doctor Edward Jenner creates the first vaccine. It's a shot to prevent a serious illness called smallpox.

DANGER SMALLPOX KEEP OUT

VACCINE

BUILDING STEAM

1804

English engineer Richard Trevithick builds the first steam locomotive.

1816

French physician Rene Laennec invents the stethoscope. With it, doctors can hear people's hearts and lungs better.

1804

George Cayley, an Englishman, flies the first model glider. He is later thought to be the first person to truly understand the basics of flight.

1807

American Robert Fulton improves the steamboat. Called the *Clermont*, his version opens the way for commercial steamboat travel.

ca. 1810

English merchant Peter Durand develops the idea of canning, or sealing food in airtight containers. Canning keeps food from spoiling.

1818

George Manby, an Englishman, invents the fire extinguisher.

1826

Frenchman Joseph Nicephore Niepce produces the first photograph.

1821

English physicist Michael Faraday invents the electric motor.

1826

English chemist John Walker invents the friction match. The match makes fire possible with one strike.

1824

Frenchman Louis Braille develops Braille. The system of raised dots helps blind people read and write.

SAVING TIME

1830

Barthelemy Thimonnier of France invents the first usable sewing machine.

1834

English mathematician Charles Babbage begins designing the Analytical Engine. The ideas behind the math machine will one day lead to the invention of the computer.

BABBAGE

1830

English engineer Edwin Beard Budding invents the first manual lawn mower.

1843

American Nancy Johnson invents a hand-cranked ice-cream maker. Its basic parts are still used to make ice cream today.

1831

American Cyrus McCormick invents the horse-drawn reaper. The machine speeds up grain collection. Before now, grains were cut and bundled by hand.

1838

American Samuel Morse makes improvements to the telegraph. His version, along with his communication code (Morse code), becomes the world telegraph standard.

1852

Frenchman Henri Giffard builds the world's first steerable passenger airship. It's called a dirigible.

GOING UP?

1852

American mechanic Elisha Otis invents the passenger elevator.

1859

Belgian engineer Etienne Lenoir creates the first internal combustion engine. Gas-powered engines like his will soon replace steam engines.

SIGHTS AND SOUNDS

1864

Louis Pasteur, a French chemist, develops a process now called pasteurization. It uses heat to kill bacteria in foods and liquids.

1867

English physician Joseph Lister uses carbolic acid on wounds. The acid kills germs and reduces infections during surgery.

1861

James Clerk Maxwell, a British physicist, creates the first color photograph.

1865

American scientist Thaddeus Lowe invents the ice-making machine. Food can now be stored for much longer periods of time without spoiling.

1866

Alfred Nobel, a Swedish chemist, creates dynamite.

1873

The first practical typewriter is made. Designed by American inventor Christopher Sholes, it has the same letter layout as today's computer keyboards.

1874

American farmer Joseph Glidden invents barbed wire. It protects ranchers' property in an effective, cheap way.

1879

Thomas Alva Edison invents an incandescent electric light bulb.

1876

American Alexander Graham Bell invents the telephone.

1877

American Thomas Alva Edison invents the phonograph. It's the first device to record and replay sound.

THINGS SEEN AND UNSEEN

1884

American architect William Le Baron Jenney invents a way to build skyscrapers.

1886

American Josephine Cochrane invents a dishwasher similar to those used today.

1891

Nikola Tesla, a Serbian-American, invents the Tesla coil. This device will be key to the invention of modern radio.

1888

American John J. Loud invents the ballpoint pen.

1886

German engineer Karl Benz builds the first useful, gasoline-powered car. It has three wheels.

1896

American inventor George Washington Carver starts developing uses for peanuts. He will invent more than 300, including soaps, dyes, and paints.

1895

Auguste and Louis Lumiere, French brothers, create the first practical movie camera/projector.

1893

American engineer George Ferris invents the Ferris wheel.

1895

German physicist Wilhelm Roentgen discovers X-ray photography. X-rays give doctors an easy way to see inside a body.

IN THE SKY, ON THE ROAD

1903

Brothers Wilbur and Orville Wright fly the first airplane at Kitty Hawk, North Carolina, on December 17. The Age of Flight begins.

1902

American inventor Willis Carrier designs the first air conditioner.

1908

American engineer Alva Fisher invents the washing machine.

1903

American inventor Mary Anderson invents the windshield wiper.

1908

The Ford Motor Company rolls out the first Model T on October 1. The car opens the way for affordable personal transportation.

1913

American automaker Henry Ford starts the first moving assembly line. Cars can now be made more quickly and for less money.

1922

Herbert Kalmus and his team at the Technicolor Motion Picture Corporation invent color movies.

FILMED IN
WONDER
COLOR

1922

Swedish scientists Baltzar von Platen and Carl Munters invent the refrigerator.

MILK

1913

Swedish-born inventor Gideon Sundback invents the zipper.

LIFESAVERS

1927

American inventor Philo Farnsworth invents the first all-electronic, black-and-white TV.

1923

American inventor Garrett Morgan designs the traffic signal.

1923

American Lee De Forest brings sound to movies.

1926

German inventor Edmund Germer invents the fluorescent light bulb. It's cooler and cheaper to use than incandescent lights.

1928

Scottish biologist Sir Alexander Fleming discovers penicillin. It is the first drug widely used to kill bacteria.

1939

Russian-American inventor Igor Sikorsky creates the first practical helicopter. All future helicopters will be modeled on it.

1935

Robert Watson-Watt, a Scottish physicist, invents radar.

1938

American engineer Alfred J. Gross invents the walkie-talkie.

1930

Ruth Graves Wakefield, an American innkeeper, bakes the first chocolate-chip cookies.

Well-Known
Ruth's

Toll House
Chocolate
Chip Cookies

23

IN LIVING COLOR

1940

Peter Goldmark, a Hungarian-American, invents the first color TV. The first sets aren't available to the public until 1951.

1946

American Marion Donovan creates the disposable diaper. The "Boater" appears in stores in 1949.

1945

American engineer Percy Spencer invents the microwave oven.

1945

A group of scientists from the U.S. Manhattan Project builds the world's first atomic bomb.

1947

American scientists John Bardeen, William Shockley, and Walter Brattain invent the transistor. It's the key to future computer technology.

1952

Jonas Salk, an American doctor, develops a vaccine against a crippling illness called polio. It will be approved for public use in 1955.

1956

Thomas Chang, a Canadian researcher, invents artificial blood.

1949

British engineer R.E. Bishop and his team develop the first jet airliner. The de Havilland Comet takes off on July 27.

1950

American Frank McNamara creates the first credit card. Called Diners Club, it's accepted at only 14 restaurants in New York City to start.

1958

Danish carpenter Ole Kirk Christensen invents LEGO blocks.

GETTING TECHNICAL

1960

American researcher Theodore Maiman invents a laser. The device directs energy with pinpoint accuracy.

1965

American chemist Stephanie Kwolek invents Kevlar. The strong material is used to make bulletproof vests.

1968

German-American inventor Ralph H. Baer develops the first video game box. Called the "Brown Box," it hooks up to a TV.

1962

On July 10, AT&T launches *Telstar 1*, a communications satellite. It sends the first TV signal through space.

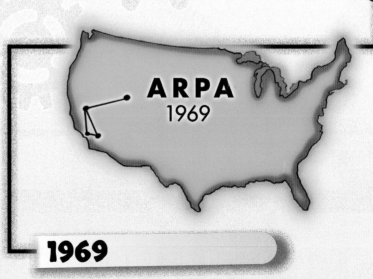

ARPA
1969

1969

The Advanced Research Project Agency (ARPA) develops the first, early form of the Internet in the United States.

1970

Amos Joel, an American engineer, invents the first cell phone technology.

1977

U.S. computer company Apple makes the first popular, mass-produced personal computer: the Apple II.

1973

Herbert Boyer and Stanley Cohen, American scientists, discover how to clone DNA in bacteria. The discovery is the start of genetic engineering.

1975

American engineer Steve Sasson invents the digital camera. It saves photos electronically, rather than on film.

CD, MMO, WWW, DVD, AND BEYOND

1979

On July 1, Sony introduces the Walkman. It's a personal portable audiocassette player.

1981

On April 12, NASA launches the space shuttle *Columbia*. It's the world's first reusable spacecraft.

1982

On August 17, the first music compact disc (CD) is produced in Germany.

1987

The first massively multiplayer online (MMO) game with graphics debuts. "Air Warrior" was developed by American designers Kelton Flinn and John Taylor.

1989

Scientists from the Fraunhofer Institute in Germany design MP3 technology. Songs and other audio can now be stored as very small digital files.

1979

George Hitchings and Gertrude Elion, American scientists, develop the first antiviral drugs. These drugs will help fight malaria, AIDS, and other diseases.

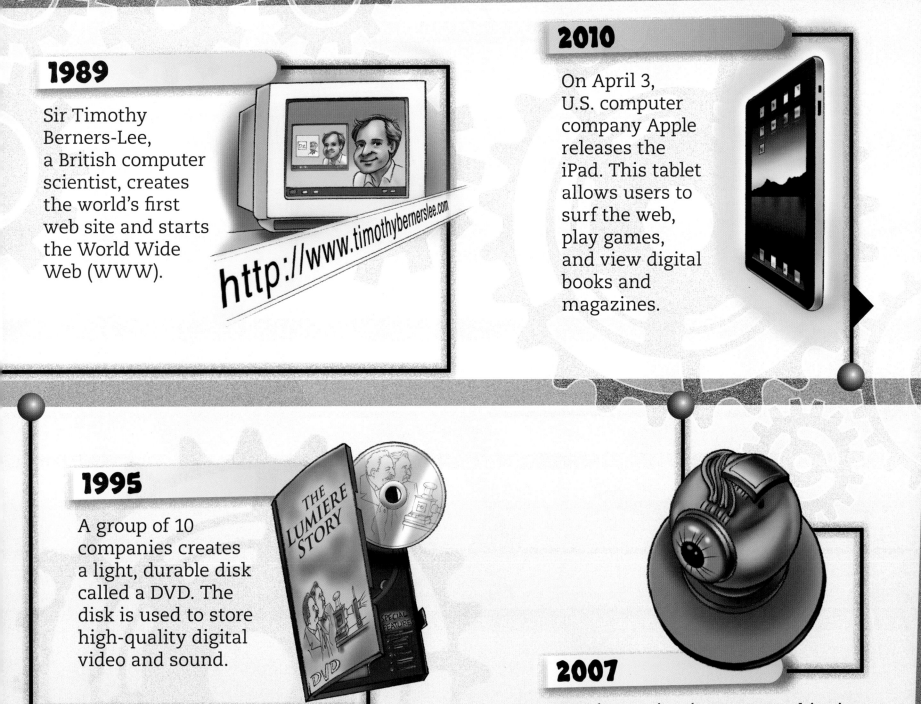

1989

Sir Timothy Berners-Lee, a British computer scientist, creates the world's first web site and starts the World Wide Web (WWW).

http://www.timothybernerslee.com

2010

On April 3, U.S. computer company Apple releases the iPad. This tablet allows users to surf the web, play games, and view digital books and magazines.

1995

A group of 10 companies creates a light, durable disk called a DVD. The disk is used to store high-quality digital video and sound.

THE LUMIERE STORY

DVD

SPECIAL FEATURES

2007

American scientists create a bionic eye that helps blind people see shapes. It's called the Argus II.

29

BUILD YOUR OWN TIMELINE

Think about objects in your home that you and your family use every day—for example, a washing machine, a microwave, or a lawn mower. Pick one and make your own timeline for it.

Start with the date the object was invented and end with present day. Keep in mind that an object may have many parts that were invented at different times. A timeline for a car, for example, may start with the invention of the wheel. Search online for dates, using search terms such as "_____ history" or "history of _____." Ask your librarian to help you find more information.

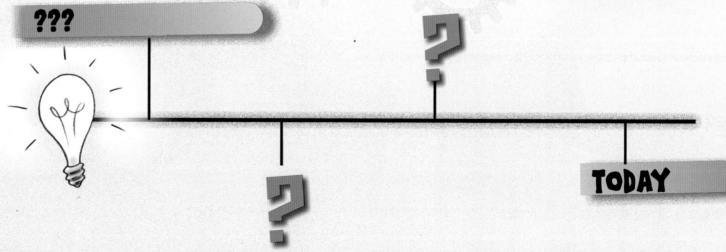

Glossary

ca.—the abbreviation for the word *circa*, which means "about" or "around"

clone—to copy

communication—the sharing of information

DNA—the bits of material that give living things their special features; the letters stand for Deoxyribo Nucleic Acid

engineer—a person who uses science to design and make things, such as machines or bridges

genetic engineering—the study of how inherited traits can be changed

incandescent—glowing with a hot, bright light

locomotive—an engine that moves on its own power

Mesopotamia—an area of southwestern Asia between the Tigris and Euphrates Rivers that includes much of present-day Iraq

phonetic—having to do with speech sounds

practical—having to do with real life

satellite—an object that orbits a planet or other space object

TO LEARN MORE

More Books to Read

Murphy, Glenn. *Inventions.* New York: Simon & Schuster Books for Young Readers, 2009.

Oxlade, Chris. *The Top Ten Inventions That Changed the World.* Top Ten. New York : PowerKids Press, 2010.

Sechrist, Darren. *Inventions and Inventors.* Graphic America. New York: Crabtree Pub., 2008.

Solway, Andrew. *Inventions and Investigations.* Sci-Hi: Physical Science. Chicago: Raintree, 2010.

Internet Sites

FactHound offers a safe, fun way to find Internet sites related to this book. All of the sites on FactHound have been researched by our staff.

Here's all you do:

Visit *www.facthound.com*

Type in this code: 9781404866621

Check out projects, games and lots more at
www.capstonekids.com

INDEX

Look for all the books in the series:

An Illustrated Timeline of Inventions and Inventors

An Illustrated Timeline of Transportation

An Illustrated Timeline of Space Exploration

An Illustrated Timeline of U.S. States